Table of Contents

26

14

18

36

22

8

30

40

Introduction

The quilts in *Quilted Living* were inspired by my newest fabric collection, "Summer Cottage", for Red Rooster Fabrics.

"Summer Cottage" was designed with all things summer in mind. From the bright, clear colors of green grass, blue skies, strawberry reds, lemon yellows, blueberry blues and pristine white to the no-fuss prints, it evokes a sense of light, casual airiness, like everything summer!

I wanted to capture the essence of those same feelings in *Quilted Living* by bringing you designs that are relaxed, casual, light and airy; quilts that lend themselves to a place indoors as well as outdoors. These quilts are at home around a campfire, outdoor concert, or a picnic under an old oak tree as well as draped over a chair, across a bed or a runner down your table.

In keeping with the relaxed and casual feeling, all the designs in *Quilted Living* were created from four very simple block elements:

- Half Square Triangle
- Flying Geese
- Quick Angled Rectangle
- Square in a Square

I love these block elements because individually or collectively they offer so many design possibilities and block creations! Come along and peruse the pages with me to see what I mean.

Half Square Triangle

Flying Geese

Quick Angled Rectangle

Square in a Square

The pinwheel takes on a new, updated look in our Tumble design found on page 8. The Tumble block uses half square triangles, flying geese and quick angled rectangles that give the block mobility to tumble across the quilt.

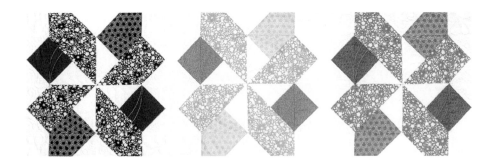

Study the effect of Basketweave on page 14. The simple placement of two flying geese on either side of a quick angled rectangle gives the illusion the block is set on point, but it's not.

X-ceptional on page 18 is just that! Partial square in a square units, quick angled rectangles and half square triangles hit the mark in this fun and exceptional design.

Who knew that a simple quick angled rectangle block could create an entire quilt? You have to see it to believe it. Just look at Streamers on page 22!

It's hard for me to design a quilt without a single star. It's even harder not to fill up an entire quilt with stars. I've been known to do that a time or two. How could I write a book without the inclusion of stars? I can't! I sprinkled them liberally in Freedom on page 26, Liberty on page 30, Stars and Stripes on page 36 and Bursting Star boxed pillow cushion on page 40. Are you seeing stars now?

Liberty Quilt   Freedom Quilt   Stars and Stripes Quilt

When it comes to the Stars and Stripes quilt, you'll be asking yourself, "What came first, the table runners or the quilt?" If you look closely at the pattern instructions for each, you may find the answer, or it may remain a debated question. I don't want to leave you in suspense, so I'll let you know that the table runners inspired the quilts. The combination of the Freedom and Liberty table runners was the sole inspiration behind Stars and Stripes!

Do you love the Bursting Star boxed pillow cushion on page 40, but don't have a need for something so large for your floor or chair? No worries, skip right through the pillow cushion construction directions and simply quilt and bind the 26" square block for a beautiful and striking wall quilt. It's that versatile!

Have you figured out which project you want to start first? Grab a tall cool glass of lemonade or ice tea (or an Arnold Palmer, if you please) and meet me on the banks of the river. Let me know which designs inspire you to live a casual, comfortable quilted life!

Cheers!

Gerri

Summer Cottage Fabric Swatches

25179-MUL

25179-RED

25179-YEL

25180-MUL

25181-BLU

25181-DKBLU

25181-GRE

25181-RED

25181-WHITE

25181-YEL

25182-DKBLU

25182-GRE

25182-LTBLU

25182-RED

25182-YEL

25183-DKBLU

25183-GRE

25183-MDBLU

25183-RED

25183-YEL

25184-GRE

25184-RED

25184-YEL

RED ROOSTER
FABRICS

When it comes to summer, we all have our favorite places to visit, foods we like to eat and things we like to do. Quilting is no different. We all have our favorite tools we like to use to speed up the process of creating our blocks. Although the instructions in *Quilted Living* do not mention specific tools or techniques, I do have my favorite go-to tools.

Alphabitties Fabric Markers

Alphabitties are adorable plastic squares perfect for labeling your fabric pieces after cutting. They are a must-have for all the designs in *Quilted Living*. I know how much you'll love them, and that's why all the cut fabric pieces in *Quilted Living* have been assigned a letter in the fabric requirements and cutting instructions. Cut, label and start sewing. Once you've used Alphabitties, you won't sew without them!

Easy Angle Ruler

There are so many different tools in the marketplace to help in the construction of half square triangles. I think I've tried just about all of them. Once I was shown how to use the Easy Angle Ruler, I never picked up another tool for the task. The Easy Angle Ruler had me at "strips right sides together, cut, sew, press and done". I've never looked back!

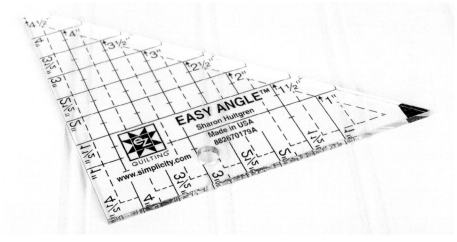

Creative Grids Rulers

If you quilt, you must have a good ruler! All of my go-to rulers are from the Creative Grids family. Embedded gripper dots with easy-to-read black and white markings always guarantee accuracy and clarity, along with a non-slip grip. I have yet to find any other ruler that has all three of these features!

WOF - width of fabric
LOF - length of fabric

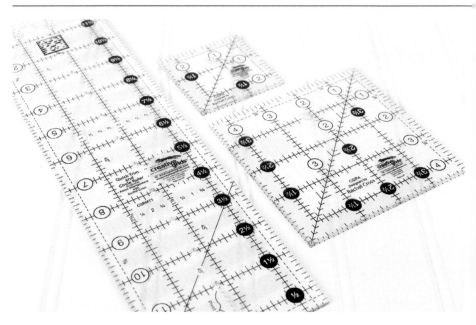

Aurifil Thread

I'm not sure why it took me so long to try Aurifil thread, but once I did, there was never another thread for me.

Aurifil 50 weight is truly the best piecing and appliqué thread on the market! In addition to providing a nice flat seam every time, I have no cotton dust balls in my machine or in my sewing room. My previous thread created an unbelievable amount of cotton build up; it was crazy!

Wonder Clips

Where do I even begin to talk about my love of these little gems? If you quilt, you must own a minimum of 50 Wonder Clips. They're meant to replace pins in binding, but they also hold multiple, thick layers of fabric really well. You see where I'm going with this, don't you? If you sew or quilt, Wonder Clips must be in your sewing room!

Rowenta Pro Precision Steam Iron

This iron is a true workhorse! There is no wrinkle or crease that this iron cannot tackle. I was teaching a class once when a student asked me if I "pop my seams" when making pinwheel blocks. I'll be honest, I really didn't know what she was talking about and asked her to explain her question. Ladies, please believe me when I tell you this; your seams will never need "popping" if you give them a good shot of steam from your Rowenta Pro Precision Steam Iron. Your pinwheel blocks will lie nice and flat. It's that amazing! Truly a game changer, in my opinion.

Press as arrows indicate throughout the book.

Tumble

Finished Size: 68 ½" x 68 ½" • **Number of Blocks: 25** • **Finished Block Size: 12" x 12"**

FABRIC REQUIREMENTS:

Fabrics	Fabric Description (Placement)	Quantity
A, B & C	Navy, blue, yellow & green print (Center Pinwheel)	Four 1 yards
D & E	Navy, blue, yellow & green tonal (Point One)	Four ½ yards
F & G	Navy, blue, yellow & green print (Point Two)	Four ½ yards
H	Red tonal (Cornerstones)	Fat Eighth
I to Q	White tonal (Background, Sashing & Borders)	4 ⅜ yards
R	Navy tonal (Binding)	¾ yard
	Backing	4 ⅜ yards

Cutting Instructions:

Center Pinwheel	A	28 (24) - 4 ½" squares *
	B	14 (12) - 2 ½" x 4 ½" rectangles *
	C	14 (12) - 2 ½" x 4 ½" rectangles *
Point One	D	7 (6) - 4 ⅞" squares *
	E	14 (12) - 2 ½" x 4 ½" rectangles *
Point Two	F	7 (6) - 4 ⅞" squares *
	G	14 (12) - 2 ½" x 4 ½" rectangles *
Cornerstones	H	36 - 1 ½" squares
Background	I	50 - 4 ⅞" squares
	J	50 - 2 ½" squares
	K	50 - 2 ½" squares
	L	100 - 2 ½" squares
	M	100 - 2 ½" squares
	N	100 - 2 ½" squares
Sashing	O	60 - 1 ½" x 12 ½" rectangles
Borders		8 - 1 ½" x WOF strips, sew end to end and subcut into:
	P	2 - 1 ½" x 66 ½" strips
	Q	2 - 1 ½" x 68 ½" strips
Binding	R	8 - 2 ½" x WOF strips

* Navy cutting is shown in first number.
Blue, yellow and green cutting is shown in parentheses.

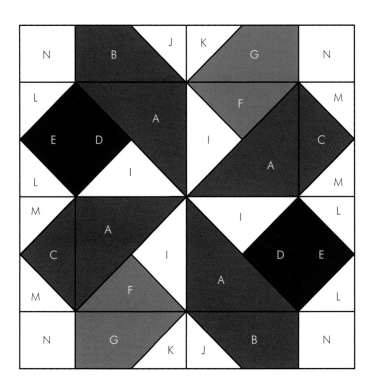

Piecing Instructions:

Tumble Blocks:

Draw a diagonal line on the wrong side of the Fabric I squares.

With right sides facing, layer a Fabric I square with a Fabric D square.

Stitch ¼" from each side of the drawn line.

Cut apart on the marked line.

Dark Half Square Triangle Unit should measure 4 ½" x 4 ½".

Make fifty.

Make fourteen.   Make twelve.

Make twelve.   Make twelve.

Draw a diagonal line on the wrong side of the Fabric A squares.

With right sides facing, layer a Fabric A square with a coordinating Dark Half Square Triangle Unit.

Pay close attention to unit placement.

Stitch on the drawn line and trim ¼" away from the seam.

Dark Tri-Tangle Unit should measure 4 ½" x 4 ½".

Make fifty.

Make fourteen.   Make twelve.

Make twelve.   Make twelve.

With right sides facing, layer a Fabric I square with a Fabric F square.

Stitch ¼" from each side of the drawn line.

Cut apart on the marked line.

Light Half Square Triangle Unit should measure 4 ½" x 4 ½".

Make fifty.

Make fourteen.   Make twelve.

Make twelve.   Make twelve.

With right sides facing, layer a Fabric A square with a coordinating Light Half Square Triangle Unit.

Pay close attention to unit placement.

Stitch on the drawn line and trim ¼" away from the seam.

Light Tri-Tangle Unit should measure 4 ½" x 4 ½".

Make fifty.

Make fourteen.   Make twelve.

Make twelve.   Make twelve.

Draw a diagonal line on the wrong side of the Fabric J squares.

With right sides facing, layer a Fabric J square on the right end of a Fabric B rectangle.

Stitch on the drawn line and trim ¼" away from the seam.

Medium Quick Angled Rectangle Unit should measure 2 ½" x 4 ½".

Make fifty.

Make fourteen.   Make twelve.

Make twelve.   Make twelve.

Draw a diagonal line on the wrong side of the Fabric K squares.

With right sides facing, layer a Fabric K square on the left end of a Fabric G rectangle.

Stitch on the drawn line and trim ¼" away from the seam.

Light Quick Angled Rectangle Unit should measure 2 ½" x 4 ½".

Make fifty.

Make fourteen.   Make twelve.

Make twelve.   Make twelve.

Assemble two Fabric N squares, one Medium Quick Angled Rectangle Unit and one coordinating Light Quick Angled Rectangle Unit.

Outside Tumble Unit should measure 2 ½" x 12 ½".

Make fifty.

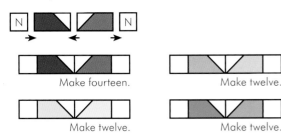
Make fourteen.   Make twelve.
Make twelve.   Make twelve.

Draw a diagonal line on the wrong side of the Fabric M squares.

With right sides facing, layer a Fabric M square on one end of a Fabric C rectangle.

Stitch on the drawn line and trim ¼" away from the seam.

Make fourteen.   Make twelve.

Make twelve.   Make twelve.

Repeat on the opposite end of the Fabric C rectangle.

Medium Flying Geese Unit should measure 2 ½" x 4 ½".

Make fifty.

Make fourteen.   Make twelve.

Make twelve.   Make twelve.

Draw a diagonal line on the wrong side of the Fabric L squares.

With right sides facing, layer a Fabric L square on one end of a Fabric E rectangle.

Stitch on the drawn line and trim ¼" away from the seam.

Make fourteen.   Make twelve.

Make twelve.   Make twelve.

Repeat on the opposite end of the Fabric E rectangle.

Dark Flying Geese Unit should measure 2 ½" x 4 ½".

Make fifty.

Make fourteen.   Make twelve.

Make twelve.   Make twelve.

Assemble one Dark Flying Geese Unit, one coordinating Dark Tri-Tangle Unit, one coordinating Light Tri-Tangle Unit and one coordinating Medium Flying Geese Unit.

Pay close attention to unit placement.

Inside Tumble Unit should measure 4 ½" x 12 ½".

Make fifty.

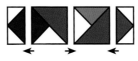

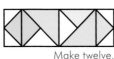 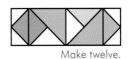
Make fourteen.   Make twelve.
Make twelve.   Make twelve.

Assemble two matching Outside Tumble Units and two matching Inside Tumble Units.

Tumble Block should measure 12 ½" x 12 ½".

Make twenty-five.

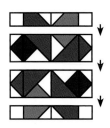 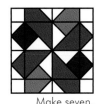 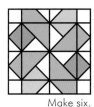 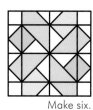 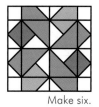

Make seven.   Make six.   Make six.   Make six.

Quilt Center:

Assemble Quilt Center.

Use the Fabric O rectangles for the sashing and the Fabric H squares for the cornerstones. Press toward the sashing.

Quilt Center should measure 66 ½" x 66 ½".

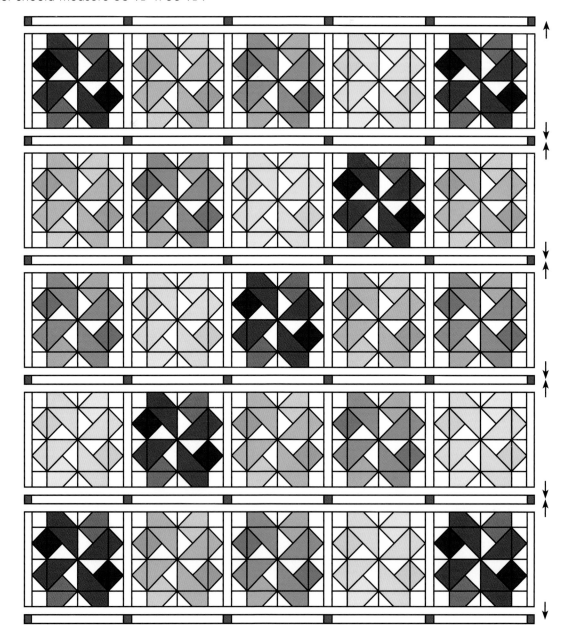

Borders:

Attach side borders using the Fabric P strips. Attach top and bottom borders using the Fabric Q strips.

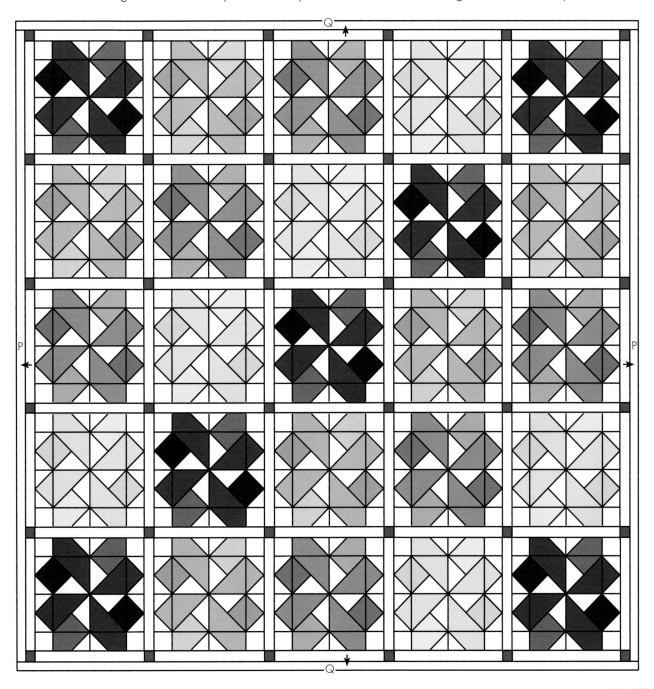

Finishing:

Sew the Fabric R strips end to end for binding.

Quilt and bind as desired.

Basketweave

Finished Size: 50 ½" x 50 ½" • Number of Blocks: 64 • Finished Block Size: 6" x 6"

FABRIC REQUIREMENTS:

Fabrics	Fabric Description (Placement)	Quantity
A & B	Assorted prints (Basketweave Blocks)	Eighteen Fat Quarters
C to G	White tonal (Background & Borders)	2 ¾ yards
H	Red tonal (Binding)	⅝ yard
	Backing	3 ⅜ yards

Cutting Instructions:

Basketweave Blocks	A	4 - 2 ½" x 6 ½" rectangles *
	B	8 - 2 ½" x 4 ½" rectangles *
Background	C	128 - 2 ½" squares
	D	256 - 2 ½" squares
	E	128 - 2 ½" squares
Borders		6 - 1 ½" x WOF strips, sew end to end and subcut into:
	F	2 - 1 ½" x 48 ½" strips
	G	2 - 1 ½" x 50 ½" strips
Binding	H	7 - 2 ½" x WOF strips

From each fat quarter.

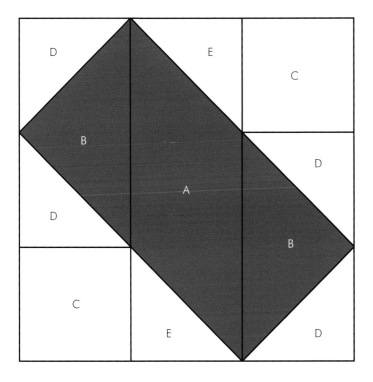

Piecing Instructions:

Basketweave Blocks:

From eight fat quarters, set aside one Fabric A rectangle and two Fabric B rectangles. These will not be used.

Draw a diagonal line on the wrong side of the Fabric D squares.

With right sides facing, layer a Fabric D square on one end of a Fabric B rectangle.

Stitch on the drawn line and trim ¼" away from the seam.

Make one hundred twenty-eight.

Repeat on the opposite end of the Fabric B rectangle.

Flying Geese Unit should measure 2 ½" x 4 ½".

Make one hundred twenty-eight.

Make one hundred twenty-eight.

Draw a diagonal line on the wrong side of the Fabric E squares.

With right sides facing, layer a Fabric E square on the top end of a Fabric A rectangle.

Stitch on the drawn line and trim ¼" away from the seam.

Make sixty-four.

Repeat on the bottom end of the Fabric A rectangle.

Quick Angled Rectangle Unit should measure 2 ½" x 6 ½".

Make sixty-four.

Make sixty-four.

Assemble one Flying Geese Unit and one Fabric C square.

Outer Basketweave Unit should measure 2 ½" x 6 ½".

Make one hundred twenty-eight.

Make one hundred twenty-eight.

Assemble two matching Outer Basketweave Units and one matching Quick Angled Rectangle Unit.

Basketweave Block should measure 6 ½" x 6 ½".

Make sixty-four.

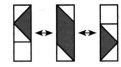

Make sixty-four.

Quilt Center:

Assemble Quilt Center.

Press rows in alternating directions.

Quilt Center should measure 48 ½" x 48 ½".

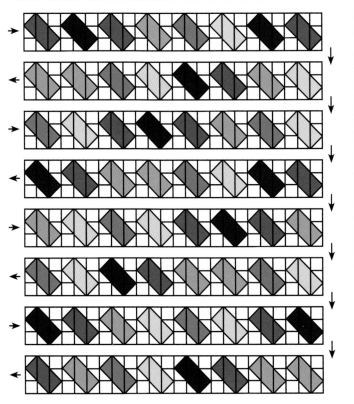

Borders:

Attach side borders using the Fabric F strips.

Attach top and bottom borders using the Fabric G strips.

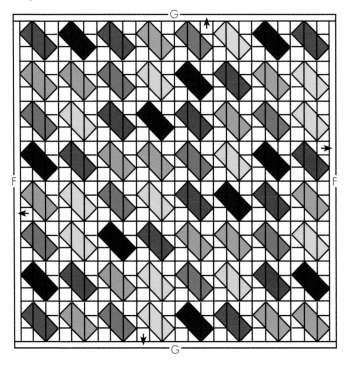

Finishing:

Sew the Fabric H strips end to end for binding.

Quilt and bind as desired.

X-ceptional

FABRIC REQUIREMENTS:

Fabrics	Fabric Description (Placement)	Quantity
A to E	Assorted prints (X-ceptional Blocks and Cornerstones)	Seven ½ yards & Eleven Fat Quarters
F to L	White tonal (Background, Sashing & Borders)	5 ⅛ yards
M	Navy tonal (Binding)	¾ yard
	Backing	4 ¼ yards

Cutting Instructions:

X-ceptional Blocks	A	4 (2) - 2 ⅞" squares *
	B	8 (4) - 2 ½" x 4 ½" rectangles *
	C	8 (4) - 2 ½" x 4 ½" rectangles *
	D	24 (12) - 2 ½" squares *
Cornerstones	E	1 (1) - 1 ½" square *
Background	F	100 - 4 ½" squares
	G	50 - 2 ⅞" squares
	H	200 - 2 ½" squares
	I	200 - 2 ½" squares
Sashing	J	40 - 1 ½" x 12 ½" rectangles
Borders		8 - 1 ½" x WOF strips, sew end to end and subcut into:
	K	2 - 1 ½" x 64 ½" strips
	L	2 - 1 ½" x 66 ½" strips
Binding	M	8 - 2 ½" x WOF strips

* ½ yard cutting is shown in first number.
  Fat quarter cutting is shown in parentheses.

Piecing Instructions:

X-ceptional Blocks:

Set aside two Fabric E squares. These will not be used.

Draw a diagonal line on the wrong side of the Fabric G squares.

With right sides facing, layer a Fabric G square with a Fabric A square.

Stitch ¼" from each side of the drawn line.

Cut apart on the marked line.

Half Square Triangle Unit should measure 2 ½" x 2 ½".

Make one hundred.

Make one hundred.

Assemble four matching Half Square Triangle Units.

Pinwheel Unit should measure 4 ½" x 4 ½".

Make twenty-five.

Make twenty-five.

Draw a diagonal line on the wrong side of the Fabric H squares.

With right sides facing, layer a Fabric H square on the top end of a Fabric B rectangle.

Stitch on the drawn line and trim ¼" away from the seam.

Make one hundred.

Repeat on the bottom end of the Fabric B rectangle.

Left Quick Angled Rectangle Unit should measure 2 ½" x 4 ½".

Make one hundred.

Make one hundred.

Draw a diagonal line on the wrong side of the Fabric I squares.

With right sides facing, layer a Fabric I square on the top end of a Fabric C rectangle.

Stitch on the drawn line and trim ¼" away from the seam.

Make one hundred.

Repeat on the bottom end of the Fabric C rectangle.

Right Quick Angled Rectangle Unit should measure 2 ½" x 4 ½".

Make one hundred.

Make one hundred.

Assemble one Left Quick Angled Rectangle Unit and one matching Right Quick Angled Rectangle Unit.

Arrow Unit should measure 4 ½" x 4 ½".

Make one hundred.

Make one hundred.

Draw a diagonal line on the wrong side of the Fabric D squares.

With right sides facing, layer a Fabric D square on the top left corner of a Fabric F square.

Stitch on the drawn line and trim ¼" away from the seam.

Make one hundred.

Repeat on the top right and bottom left corners of the Fabric F square with matching Fabric D squares.

Partial Square in a Square Unit should measure 4 ½" x 4 ½".

Make one hundred.

Make one hundred.

Assemble four matching Partial Square in a Square Units, four matching Arrow Units and one matching Pinwheel Unit.

X-ceptional Block should measure 12 ½" x 12 ½".

Make twenty-five.

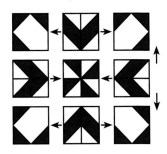

Make twenty-five.

Quilt Center:

Assemble Quilt Center.

Use the Fabric J rectangles for the sashing and the Fabric E squares for the cornerstones. Press toward the sashing.

Quilt Center should measure 64 ½" x 64 ½".

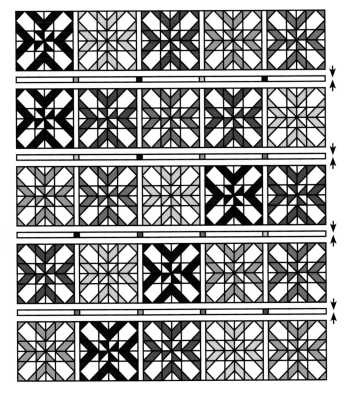

Borders:

Attach side borders using the Fabric K strips.

Attach top and bottom borders using the Fabric L strips.

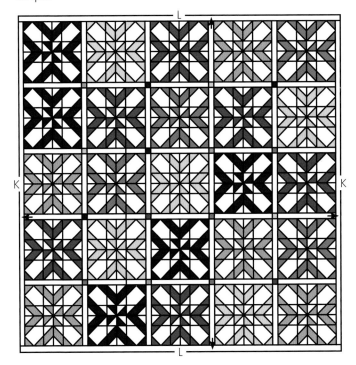

Finishing:

Sew the Fabric M strips end to end for binding.

Quilt and bind as desired.

Streamers

Finished Size: 52 ½" x 68 ½" • Number of Blocks: 24 • Finished Block Size: 8" x 16"

FABRIC REQUIREMENTS:

Fabrics	Fabric Description (Placement)	Quantity
A & B	Assorted prints (Streamers Blocks)	Eighteen Fat Quarters
C to H	White tonal (Background & Borders)	4 yards
I	Red tonal (Binding)	⅝ yard
	Backing	4 ⅜ yards

Cutting Instructions:

Streamers Blocks	A	6 - 2 ½" x 4 ½" rectangles *
	B	6 - 2 ½" x 4 ½" rectangles *
Background	C	24 - 4 ½" x 8 ½" rectangles
	D	96 - 2 ½" x 4 ½" rectangles
	E	192 - 2 ½" squares
	F	192 - 2 ½" squares
Borders		7 - 2 ½" x WOF strips, sew end to end and subcut into:
	G	2 - 2 ½" x 64 ½" strips
	H	2 - 2 ½" x 52 ½" strips
Binding	I	7 - 2 ½" x WOF strips

From each fat quarter.

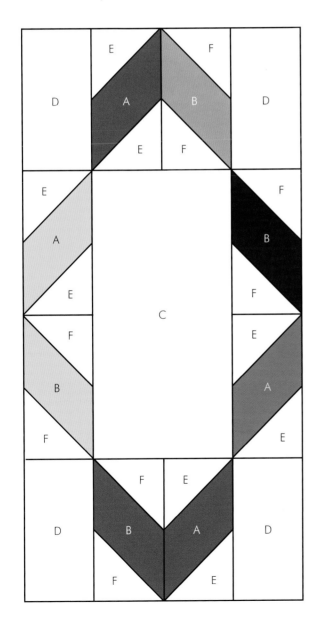

Piecing Instructions:

Streamers Blocks:

Set aside twelve Fabric A rectangles and twelve Fabric B rectangles. These will not be used.

Draw a diagonal line on the wrong side of the Fabric E squares.

With right sides facing, layer a Fabric E square on the top end of a Fabric A rectangle.

Stitch on the drawn line and trim ¼" away from the seam.

Make ninety-six.

Repeat on the bottom end of the Fabric A rectangle.

Left Quick Angled Rectangle Unit should measure 2 ½" x 4 ½".

Make ninety-six.

Make ninety-six.

Draw a diagonal line on the wrong side of the Fabric F squares.

With right sides facing, layer a Fabric F square on the top end of a Fabric B rectangle.

Stitch on the drawn line and trim ¼" away from the seam.

Make ninety-six.

Repeat on the bottom end of the Fabric B rectangle.

Right Quick Angled Rectangle Unit should measure 2 ½" x 4 ½".

Make ninety-six.

Make ninety-six.

Assemble two Fabric D rectangles, one Left Quick Angled Rectangle Unit and one Right Quick Angled Rectangle Unit.

Outer Streamers Unit should measure 4 ½" x 8 ½".

Make forty-eight.

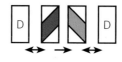

Make forty-eight.

Assemble two Left Quick Angled Rectangle Units, two Right Quick Angled Rectangle Units and one Fabric C rectangle.

Inner Streamers Unit should measure 8 ½" x 8 ½".

Make twenty-four.

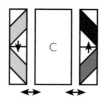

Make twenty-four.

Assemble two Outer Streamers Units and one Inner Streamers Unit.

Streamers Block should measure 8 ½" x 16 ½".

Make twenty-four.

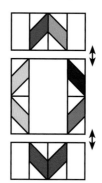 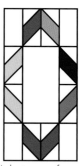

Make twenty-four.

Quilt Center:

Assemble Quilt Center.

Press rows in alternating directions.

Quilt Center should measure 48 ½" x 64 ½".

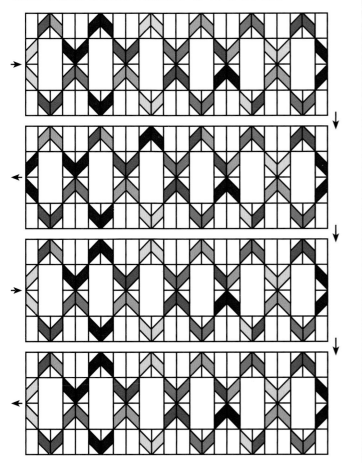

Borders:

Attach side borders using the Fabric G strips.

Attach top and bottom borders using the Fabric H strips.

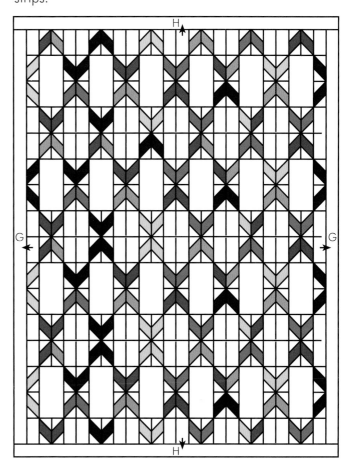

Finishing:

Sew the Fabric I strips end to end for binding.

Quilt and bind as desired.

Freedom

FABRIC REQUIREMENTS:

Fabrics	Fabric Description (Placement)	Throw	Table Runner
A & B	Assorted red prints (Star Blocks)	(1) ⅞ yard (2) ⅝ yards	(1) ½ yard (2) ⅓ yards
C	Navy tonal (Arrow Blocks)	1 ½ yards	⅝ yard
D	Navy print (Arrow Blocks)	1 ½ yards	⅝ yard
E to G	White tonal (Background)	4 yards	1 ⅝ yards
H	Red tonal (Binding)	¾ yard	½ yard
	Backing	4 ⅝ yards	1 ⅞ yards

Throw Cutting Instructions:

Star Blocks	A	12 (8) - 4 ½" squares *
	B	96 (64) - 2 ½" squares *
Arrow Blocks	C	35 - 4 ½" x 8 ½" rectangles
Arrow Blocks	D	35 - 4 ½" x 8 ½" rectangles
Background	E	140 - 4 ½" squares
	F	112 - 2 ½" x 4 ½" rectangles
	G	112 - 2 ½" squares
Binding	H	8 - 2 ½" x WOF strips

* ⅞ yard cutting is shown in first number.
   ⅝ yard cutting is shown in parentheses.

Table Runner Cutting Instructions:

Star Blocks	A	3 (2) - 4 ½" squares *
	B	24 (16) - 2 ½" squares *
Arrow Blocks	C	14 - 4 ½" x 8 ½" rectangles
Arrow Blocks	D	14 - 4 ½" x 8 ½" rectangles
Background	E	56 - 4 ½" squares
	F	28 - 2 ½" x 4 ½" rectangles
	G	28 - 2 ½" squares
Binding	H	5 - 2 ½" x WOF strips

* ½ yard cutting is shown in first number.
   ⅓ yard cutting is shown in parentheses.

Piecing Instructions:

Arrow Blocks:

With right sides facing, layer a Fabric E square on the top end of a Fabric D rectangle.

Stitch on the drawn line and trim ¼" away from the seam.

Repeat on the bottom end of the Fabric D rectangle.

Left Quick Angled Rectangle Unit should measure 4 ½" x 8 ½".

Throw:
Make thirty-five.

Table Runner:
Make fourteen.

Draw a diagonal line on the wrong side of the Fabric E squares.

With right sides facing, layer a Fabric E square on the top end of a Fabric C rectangle.

Stitch on the drawn line and trim ¼" away from the seam.

Repeat on the bottom end of the Fabric C rectangle.

Right Quick Angled Rectangle Unit should measure 4 ½" x 8 ½".

Throw:
Make thirty-five.

Table Runner:
Make fourteen.

Assemble one Left Quick Angled Rectangle Unit and one Right Quick Angled Rectangle Unit.

Arrow Block should measure 8 ½" x 8 ½".

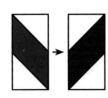

Throw:
Make thirty-five.

Table Runner:
Make fourteen.

Star Blocks:

Draw a diagonal line on the wrong side of the Fabric B squares.

With right sides facing, layer a Fabric B square on one end of a Fabric F rectangle.

Stitch on the drawn line and trim ¼" away from the seam.

Repeat on the opposite end of the Fabric F rectangle with a matching Fabric B square.

Flying Geese Unit should measure 2 ½" x 4 ½".

Throw:
Make one hundred twelve.

Table Runner:
Make twenty-eight.

Assemble four Fabric G squares, four matching Flying Geese Units and one matching Fabric A square.

Star Block should measure 8 ½" x 8 ½".

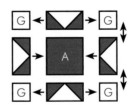

Throw:
Make twenty-eight.

Table Runner:
Make seven.

Throw Quilt Center:

Assemble Throw Quilt Center.

Press rows in alternating directions.

Throw Quilt Center should measure 56 ½" x 72 ½".

Throw Finishing:

Sew the Fabric H strips end to end for binding.

Quilt and bind as desired.

Table Runner Center:

Assemble Table Runner Center.

Press rows in alternating directions.

Table Runner Center should measure 24 ½" x 56 ½".

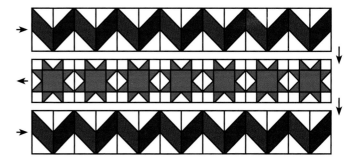

Table Runner Finishing:

Sew the Fabric H strips end to end for binding.

Quilt and bind as desired.

Liberty

Throw: 56 ½" x 66 ½" • Table Runner: 24 ½" x 56 ½"

FABRIC REQUIREMENTS:

Fabrics	Fabric Description (Placement)	Throw	Table Runner
A, B & C	Navy tonal (Star Rows)	⅝ yard	⅓ yard
D, E & F	Navy print (Star Rows)	⅝ yard	⅓ yard
G, H & I	Navy print (Star Rows)	⅝ yard	⅓ yard
J	Red tonal (Stripe Rows)	1 ⅞ yards	1 ⅞ yards
K	Red print (Stripe Rows)	1 ⅞ yards	1 ⅞ yards
L to P	White tonal (Stripe Rows & Background)	3 yards	1 ⅞ yards
Q	Navy tonal (Binding)	¾ yard	½ yard
	Backing	4 ¼ yards	1 ⅞ yards

Throw Cutting Instructions:

Star Rows	A	23 - 2 ½" squares
	B	104 - 1 ½" squares
	C	80 - 1 ½" squares
Star Rows	D	22 - 2 ½" squares
	E	96 - 1 ½" squares
	F	80 - 1 ½" squares
Star Rows	G	20 - 2 ½" squares
	H	80 - 1 ½" squares
	I	80 - 1 ½" squares
Stripe Rows	J	10 - 2 ½" x 56 ½" LOF strips
Stripe Rows	K	4 - 1 ½" x 56 ½" LOF strips
Stripe Rows	L	8 - 2" x 56 ½" LOF strips
Background	M	140 - 2 ½" squares
	N	140 - 2 ½" squares
	O	60 - 2 ½" squares
	P	10 - 1 ½" x 6 ½" rectangles
Binding	Q	8 - 2 ½" x WOF strips

Table Runner Cutting Instructions:

Star Rows	A	9 - 2 ½" squares
	B	40 - 1 ½" squares
	C	32 - 1 ½" squares
Star Rows	D	8 - 2 ½" squares
	E	32 - 1 ½" squares
	F	32 - 1 ½" squares
Star Rows	G	9 - 2 ½" squares
	H	40 - 1 ½" squares
	I	32 - 1 ½" squares
Stripe Rows	J	4 - 2 ½" x 56 ½" LOF strips
Stripe Rows	K	1 - 1 ½" x 56 ½" LOF strips
Stripe Rows	L	2 - 2" x 56 ½" LOF strips
Background	M	56 - 2 ½" squares
	N	56 - 2 ½" squares
	O	24 - 2 ½" squares
	P	4 - 1 ½" x 6 ½" rectangles
Binding	Q	5 - 2 ½" x WOF strips

Piecing Instructions:

Star Units:

Draw a diagonal line on the wrong side of the Fabric B squares.

With right sides facing, layer a Fabric B square on the bottom left corner of a Fabric N square.

Stitch on the drawn line and trim ¼" away from the seam.

Repeat on the bottom right corner of the Fabric N square.

Star Tip Unit One should measure 2 ½" x 2 ½".

Throw:
Make fifty-two.

Table Runner:
Make twenty.

Draw a diagonal line on the wrong side of the Fabric E squares.

With right sides facing, layer a Fabric E square on the bottom left corner of a Fabric N square.

Stitch on the drawn line and trim ¼" away from the seam.

Repeat on the bottom right corner of the Fabric N square.

Star Tip Unit Two should measure 2 ½" x 2 ½".

Throw:
Make forty-eight.

Table Runner:
Make sixteen.

Draw a diagonal line on the wrong side of the Fabric H squares.

With right sides facing, layer a Fabric H square on the bottom left corner of a Fabric N square.

Stitch on the drawn line and trim ¼" away from the seam.

Repeat on the bottom right corner of the Fabric N square.

Star Tip Unit Three should measure 2 ½" x 2 ½".

Throw:
Make forty.

Table Runner:
Make twenty.

Draw a diagonal line on the wrong side of the Fabric C and the Fabric F squares.

With right sides facing, layer a Fabric C square on the top left corner and a Fabric F square on the bottom right corner of a Fabric O square.

Stitch on the drawn line and trim ¼" away from the seam.

Repeat on the bottom left corner with a Fabric C square and the top right corner with a Fabric F square.

Square in a Square Unit One should measure 2 ½" x 2 ½".

Throw:
Make twenty.

Table Runner:
Make eight.

Draw a diagonal line on the wrong side of the Fabric I squares.

With right sides facing, layer a Fabric F square on the top left corner and a Fabric I square on the bottom right corner of a Fabric O square.

Stitch on the drawn line and trim ¼" away from the seam.

Repeat on the bottom left corner with a Fabric F square and the top right corner with a Fabric I square.

Square in a Square Unit Two should measure 2 ½" x 2 ½".

Throw:
Make twenty.

Table Runner:
Make eight.

With right sides facing, layer a Fabric I square on the top left corner and a Fabric C square on the bottom right corner of a Fabric O square.

Stitch on the drawn line and trim ¼" away from the seam.

Repeat on the bottom left corner with a Fabric I square and the top right corner with a Fabric C square.

Square in a Square Unit Three should measure 2 ½" x 2 ½".

Throw:
Make twenty.

Table Runner:
Make eight.

Assemble two Fabric M squares and one Star Tip Unit One.

Star Row Unit One should measure 2 ½" x 6 ½".

Throw:
Make six.

Table Runner:
Make two.

Assemble two Fabric M squares and one Star Tip Unit Two.

Star Row Unit Two should measure 2 ½" x 6 ½".

Throw:
Make four.

Table Runner:
Make zero.

Assemble two Fabric M squares and one Star Tip Unit Three.

Star Row Unit Three should measure 2 ½" x 6 ½".

Throw:
Make zero.

Table Runner:
Make two.

Assemble two Star Tip Unit Ones and one Fabric A square.

Star Row Unit Four should measure 2 ½" x 6 ½".

Throw:
Make twenty-three.

Table Runner:
Make nine.

Assemble two Star Tip Unit Twos and one Fabric D square.

Star Row Unit Five should measure 2 ½" x 6 ½".

Throw:
Make twenty-two.

Table Runner:
Make eight.

Assemble two Star Tip Unit Threes and one Fabric G square.

Star Row Unit Six should measure 2 ½" x 6 ½".

Throw:
Make twenty.

Table Runner:
Make nine.

Assemble two Fabric M squares and one Square in a Square Unit One.

Pay close attention to unit placement.

Star Row Unit Seven should measure 2 ½" x 6 ½".

Throw:
Make twenty.

Table Runner:
Make eight.

Assemble two Fabric M squares and one Square in a Square Unit Two.

Pay close attention to unit placement.

Star Row Unit Eight should measure 2 ½" x 6 ½".

Throw:
Make twenty.

Table Runner:
Make eight.

Assemble two Fabric M squares and one Square in a Square Unit Three.

Pay close attention to unit placement.

Star Row Unit Nine should measure 2 ½" x 6 ½".

Throw:
Make twenty.

Table Runner:
Make eight.

Star Rows:

Assemble Star Rows.

Press each row to the right.

Star Row should measure 6 ½" x 56 ½".

Throw:
Make three.

Table Runner:
Make one.

Throw:
Make two.

Table Runner:
Make zero.

Throw:
Make zero.

Table Runner:
Make one.

Stripe Rows:

Assemble two Fabric J strips, two Fabric L strips and one Fabric K strip.

Stripe Row should measure 8 ½" x 56 ½".

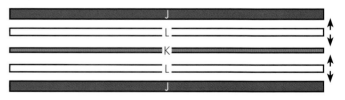

Throw:
Make four.

Table Runner:
Make one.

Throw Quilt Center:

Assemble Throw Quilt Center.

Throw Quilt Center should measure 56 ½" x 66 ½".

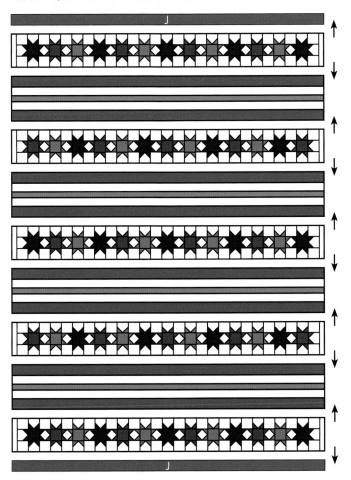

Throw Finishing:

Sew the Fabric Q strips end to end for binding.

Quilt and bind as desired.

Table Runner Center:

Assemble Table Runner Center.

Table Runner Center should measure 24 ½" x 56 ½".

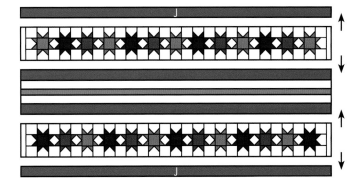

Table Runner Finishing:

Sew the Fabric Q strips end to end for binding.

Quilt and bind as desired.

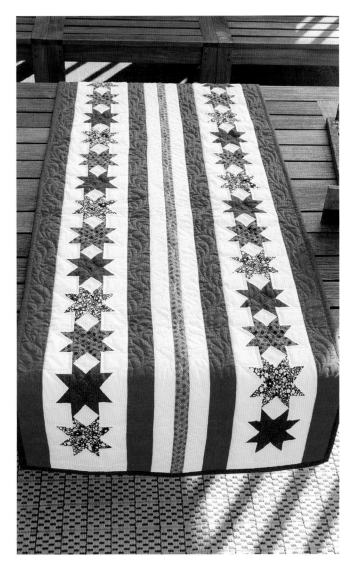

Stars and Stripes

Finished Size: 56 ½" x 72 ½"

FABRIC REQUIREMENTS:

Freedom Table Runner	Liberty Table Runner	Fabric Description (Placement)	Quantity
A & B	K	Red print (Star Blocks & Stripe Rows)	2 ¼ yards
A & B	-	Red print (Star Blocks)	½ yard
A & B	J	Red tonal (Star Blocks & Stripe Rows)	2 ¼ yards
C	A, B & C	Navy tonal (Arrow Blocks & Star Rows)	1 ⅓ yards
D	D, E & F	Navy print (Arrow Blocks & Star Rows)	1 ⅓ yards
-	G, H & I	Navy print (Star Rows)	⅓ yard
E to G	L to P	White tonal (Background & Stripe Rows)	4 ⅜ yards
		Red tonal (Binding)	¾ yard
		Backing	4 ⅝ yards

This quilt is made by assembling three table runners.
Follow the cutting instructions below.

Freedom Table Runner
Cutting Instructions:

Star Blocks	A	6 (4) - 4 ½" squares *
	B	48 (32) - 2 ½" squares *
Arrow Blocks	C	28 - 4 ½" x 8 ½" rectangles
Arrow Blocks	D	28 - 4 ½" x 8 ½" rectangles
Background	E	112 - 4 ½" squares
	F	56 - 2 ½" x 4 ½" rectangles
	G	56 - 2 ½" squares

* 1st Star Block is shown in first number.
2nd and 3rd Star Blocks are shown in parentheses.

Liberty Table Runner
Cutting Instructions:

Star Rows	A	9 - 2 ½" squares
	B	40 - 1 ½" squares
	C	32 - 1 ½" squares
Star Rows	D	8 - 2 ½" squares
	E	32 - 1 ½" squares
	F	32 - 1 ½" squares
Star Rows	G	9 - 2 ½" squares
	H	40 - 1 ½" squares
	I	32 - 1 ½" squares
Stripe Rows	J	4 - 2 ½" x 56 ½" LOF strips
Stripe Rows	K	1 - 1 ½" x 56 ½" LOF strips
Stripe Rows	L	2 - 2" x 56 ½" LOF strips
Background	M	56 - 2 ½" squares
	N	56 - 2 ½" squares
	O	24 - 2 ½" squares
	P	4 - 1 ½" x 6 ½" rectangles

Cutting Instructions:

| Binding | | 8 - 2 ½" x WOF strips |

Piecing Instructions:

Freedom Table Runner:

Follow instructions for the Freedom Table Runner on pages 26 to 29.

When following instructions double the number of units and blocks you make.

Make two.

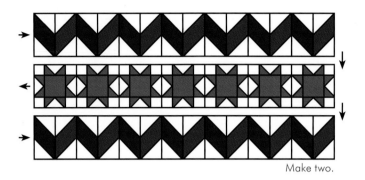

Make two.

Liberty Table Runner:

Follow instructions for the Liberty Table Runner on pages 30 to 35.

Make one.

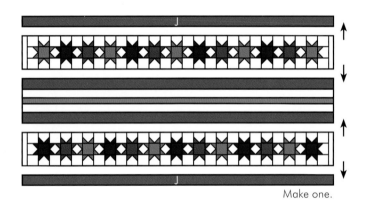

Make one.

Quilt Center:

Assemble Quilt Center.

Quilt Center should measure 56 ½" x 72 ½".

Finishing:

Sew the binding strips end to end for binding.

Quilt and bind as desired.

Bursting Star

Boxed Pillow Cushion • Finished Size: 26" x 26"

FABRIC REQUIREMENTS:

Fabrics	Fabric Description (Placement)	Quantity
A to F	Red tonal (Star Block)	⅝ yard
G to J	Navy print (Star Block)	⅜ yard
K to T	White tonal (Background & Borders)	1 ⅛ yards
U	Navy tonal (Piping)	1 yard
V & W	Red print (Boxing Strip & Pillow Backing)	1 ½ yards
	Muslin (Pillow Lining)	1 yard
	Batting	30" square
	Polyfil pillow stuffing	
	¼" diameter cotton cording	7 yards

Cutting Instructions:

Star Block	A	1 - 4 ½" square
	B	4 - 2 ⅞" squares
	C	16 - 2 ½" x 4 ½" rectangles
	D	16 - 2 ½" x 4 ½" rectangles
	E	8 - 2 ½" squares
	F	4 - 2 ½" squares
Star Block	G	4 - 2 ⅞" squares
	H	8 - 2 ½" x 4 ½" rectangles
	I	8 - 2 ½" x 4 ½" rectangles
	J	4 - 2 ½" squares
Background	K	4 - 2 ⅞" squares
	L	4 - 2 ⅞" squares
	M	4 - 2 ½" x 4 ½" rectangles
	N	32 - 2 ½" squares
	O	32 - 2 ½" squares
	P	16 - 2 ½" squares
	Q	16 - 2 ½" squares
	R	12 - 2 ½" squares
Borders	S	2 - 1 ½" x 24 ½" strips
	T	2 - 1 ½" x 26 ½" strips
Piping	U	2" bias strips (240" total)
Boxing Strip	V	3 - 5 ½" x WOF strips
Pillow Backing	W	Cut to match Quilted Cushion Top
Muslin		1 - 30" square

Piecing Instructions:

Cushion Center:

Draw a diagonal line on the wrong side of the Fabric E squares.

With right sides facing, layer a Fabric E square on one end of a Fabric M rectangle.

Stitch on the drawn line and trim ¼" away from the seam.

Make four.

Repeat on the opposite end of the Fabric M rectangle.

Flying Geese Unit should measure 2 ½" x 4 ½".

Make four.

Make four.

Assemble four Fabric R squares, four Flying Geese Units and one Fabric A square.

Center Star Unit should measure 8 ½" x 8 ½".

Make one.

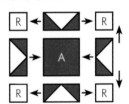

Make one.

Draw a diagonal line on the wrong side of the Fabric K squares.

With right sides facing, layer a Fabric K square with a Fabric B square.

Stitch ¼" from each side of the drawn line.

Cut apart on the marked line.

Red Half Square Triangle Unit should measure 2 ½" x 2 ½".

Make eight.

Make eight.

Assemble one Fabric R square, two Red Half Square Triangle Units and one Fabric F square.

Red Tulip Unit should measure 4 ½" x 4 ½".

Make four.

Make four.

Draw a diagonal line on the wrong side of the Fabric L squares.

With right sides facing, layer a Fabric L square with a Fabric G square.

Stitch ¼" from each side of the drawn line.

Cut apart on the marked line.

Navy Half Square Triangle Unit should measure 2 ½" x 2 ½".

Make eight.

Make eight.

Assemble one Fabric R square, two Navy Half Square Triangle Units and one Fabric J square.

Navy Tulip Unit should measure 4 ½" x 4 ½".

Make four.

Make four.

Draw a diagonal line on the wrong side of the Fabric N squares.

With right sides facing, layer a Fabric N square on the top end of a Fabric C rectangle.

Stitch on the drawn line and trim ¼" away from the seam.

Make sixteen.

Repeat on the bottom end of the Fabric C rectangle.

Left Red Quick Angled Rectangle Unit should measure 2 ½" x 4 ½".

Make sixteen.

Make sixteen.

Draw a diagonal line on the wrong side of the Fabric O squares.

With right sides facing, layer a Fabric O square on the top end of a Fabric D rectangle.

Stitch on the drawn line and trim ¼" away from the seam.

Make sixteen.

Repeat on the bottom end of the Fabric D rectangle.

Right Red Quick Angled Rectangle Unit should measure 2 ½" x 4 ½".

Make sixteen.

Make sixteen.

Draw a diagonal line on the wrong side of the Fabric P squares.

With right sides facing, layer a Fabric P square on the top end of a Fabric H rectangle.

Stitch on the drawn line and trim ¼" away from the seam.

Make eight.

Repeat on the bottom end of the Fabric H rectangle.

Left Navy Quick Angled Rectangle Unit should measure 2 ½" x 4 ½".

Make eight.

Make eight.

Draw a diagonal line on the wrong side of the Fabric Q squares.

With right sides facing, layer a Fabric Q square on the top end of a Fabric I rectangle.

Stitch on the drawn line and trim ¼" away from the seam.

Make eight.

Repeat on the bottom end of the Fabric I rectangle.

Right Navy Quick Angled Rectangle Unit should measure 2 ½" x 4 ½".

Make eight.

Make eight.

Assemble one Red Tulip Unit, two Left Red Quick Angled Rectangle Units, two Right Red Quick Angled Rectangle Units and one Navy Tulip Unit.

Pay close attention to unit placement.

Corner Star Unit should measure 8 ½" x 8 ½".

Make four.

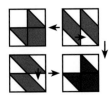

Make four.

Assemble two Left Red Quick Angled Rectangle Units, two Right Red Quick Angled Rectangle Units, two Left Navy Quick Angled Rectangle Units and two Right Navy Quick Angled Rectangle Units.

Pay close attention to unit placement.

Middle Star Unit should measure 8 ½" x 8 ½".

Make four.

Make four.

Assemble Cushion Center.

Cushion Center should measure 24 ½" x 24 ½".

Borders:

Attach side borders using the Fabric S strips.

Attach top and bottom borders using the Fabric T strips.

Cushion Top should measure 26 ½" x 26 ½".

Pillow Cushion Top:

Layer the Cushion Top, the batting and the muslin.

Quilt the Cushion Top as desired.

Baste ⅛" around the inside of the Cushion Top.

Trim excess batting and muslin at the edge of the Quilted Cushion Top.

Piping:

Sew the Fabric U strips end to end on the diagonal to make one continuous strip.

Press seams open for less bulk.

To make the Piping, fold the Fabric U strips wrong sides together lengthwise.

Place the cording inside the fold.

Use a zipper foot and move the needle to the left of the foot.

Using matching thread, sew along the edge of the cording.

Trim ¼" away from the stitch line.

Cut Piping into two 120" strips.

Layer the raw edges of the Piping strip and the Quilted Cushion Top leaving a 3" tail at the beginning.

Sew on the previously stitched line.

Backstitch at the beginning and end.

Sew to ½" away from the corner and with the needle in the down position cut three diagonal lines up to your stitch line to create a pivot point.

Continue sewing to ¼" away from the corner and pivot. Continue sewing.

When you get close to the end, trim the Piping end 1" past the starting point.

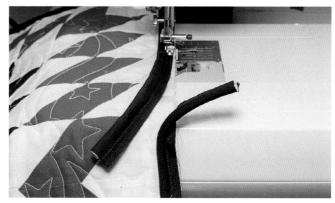

Mark the spot where the two strips meet.

Un-stitch the ending strip to the marked line to expose the cording underneath.

Line up the two strips and mark the exposed cording and the beginning Piping strip.

Cut the ending cording and the beginning Piping strip on the drawn line.

Cut the Piping fabric ½" away from the ending cording.

Tuck the Piping fabric under to hide the raw edge.

Wrap the ending Piping fabric around the beginning Piping strip to hide the cording.

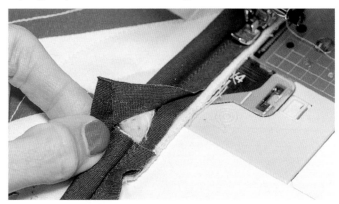

Sew the opening closed, making sure to sew over the existing stitches.

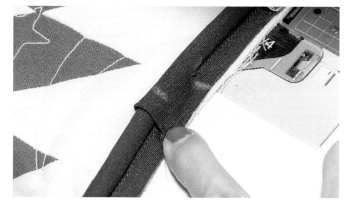

Repeat previous steps to attach Piping to the Pillow Cushion Backing.

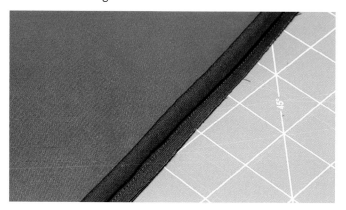

Finishing the Pillow Cushion:

Measure the outside edge of the Piping on the Pillow Cushion Top with a measuring tape and add ½" to determine the length of your Boxing Strip.

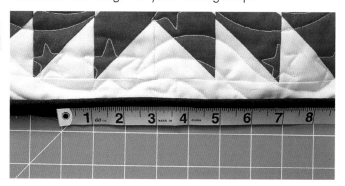

Sew the Fabric V strips end to end with a straight seam and trim to the length determined in the previous step.

Press seams open for less bulk.

Sew the ends of the Fabric V strip together to form a continuous loop.

With right sides facing, pin the raw edges of the Boxing Strip and the Pillow Cushion Top. Make sure the seams are not in the corners.

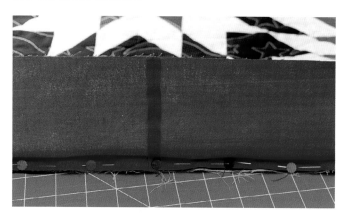

Stitch ¼" around the edge of the Cushion Top.

When you reach the first corner of the Cushion Top, stop sewing with your machine in the needle down position.

Cut a slit in the Boxing Strip almost to the needle.

Pivot and continue sewing.

Backstitch at the beginning and end.

Repeat previous steps to attach the Boxing Strip to the Pillow Cushion Back and leave an 8" opening.

Backstitch at the beginning and end.

Turn right side out.

Insert the polyfil pillow stuffing into the Bursting Star Pillow Cushion.

Stitch the opening closed.

Fabric Key

Tumble Quilt – Page 8

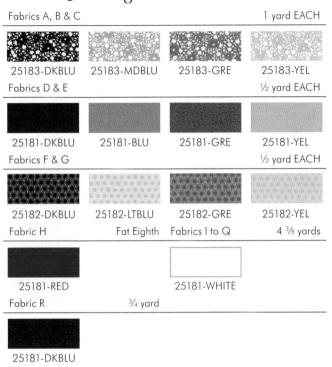

Fabrics A, B & C			1 yard EACH
25183-DKBLU	25183-MDBLU	25183-GRE	25183-YEL

Fabrics D & E			½ yard EACH
25181-DKBLU	25181-BLU	25181-GRE	25181-YEL

Fabrics F & G			½ yard EACH
25182-DKBLU	25182-LTBLU	25182-GRE	25182-YEL

Fabric H	Fat Eighth	Fabrics I to Q	4 ⅜ yards
25181-RED		25181-WHITE	

Fabric R	¾ yard
25181-DKBLU	

Backing	4 ⅜ yards

Basketweave Quilt – Page 14

Fabrics A & B			Fat Quarter EACH
25179-RED	25179-YEL	25180-MUL	25181-BLU
25181-DKBLU	25181-GRE	25181-RED	25181-YEL
25182-DKBLU	25182-GRE	25182-LTBLU	25182-RED
25182-YEL	25183-DKBLU	25183-GRE	25183-MDBLU
25183-RED	25183-YEL		

Fabrics C to G	2 ¾ yards	Fabric H	⅝ yard
25181-WHITE		25181-RED	

Backing	3 ⅜ yards

X–ceptional Quilt – Page 18

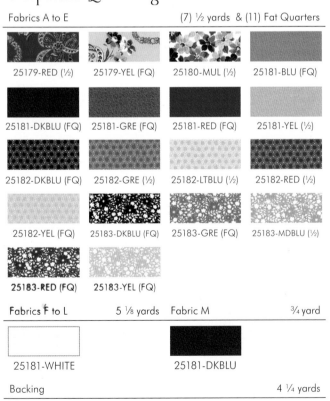

Fabrics A to E		(7) ½ yards	& (11) Fat Quarters
25179-RED (½)	25179-YEL (FQ)	25180-MUL (½)	25181-BLU (FQ)
25181-DKBLU (FQ)	25181-GRE (FQ)	25181-RED (FQ)	25181-YEL (½)
25182-DKBLU (FQ)	25182-GRE (½)	25182-LTBLU (½)	25182-RED (½)
25182-YEL (FQ)	25183-DKBLU (FQ)	25183-GRE (FQ)	25183-MDBLU (½)
25183-RED (FQ)	25183-YEL (FQ)		

Fabrics F to L	5 ⅛ yards	Fabric M	¾ yard
25181-WHITE		25181-DKBLU	

Backing	4 ¼ yards

Streamers Quilt – Page 22

Fabrics A & B			Fat Quarter EACH
25179-RED	25179-YEL	25180-MUL	25181-BLU
25181-DKBLU	25181-GRE	25181-RED	25181-YEL
25182-DKBLU	25182-GRE	25182-LTBLU	25182-RED
25182-YEL	25183-DKBLU	25183-GRE	25183-MDBLU
25183-RED	25183-YEL		

Fabrics C to H	4 yards	Fabric I	⅝ yard
25181-WHITE		25181-RED	

Backing	4 ⅜ yards